T0266123

NONE OF THIS BELONGS TO ME

NIGHTWOOD EDITIONS

2021

NONE OF THIS BELONGS TO ME

POEMS

ELLIE SAWATZKY

Nightwood Editions
P.O. Box 1779
Gibsons, BC VON 1VO
Canada
www.nightwoodeditions.com

COVER ART: WKNDRS Rachel Rivera + Claire Ouchi
COVER DESIGN: Carleton Wilson
TYPOGRAPHY: Carleton Wilson

Nightwood Editions acknowledges the support of the Canada Council for the Arts, the Government of Canada, and the Province of British Columbia through the BC Arts Council.

This book has been produced on 100% post-consumer recycled, ancient-forest-free paper, processed chlorine-free and printed with vegetable-based dyes.

Printed and bound in Canada.

LIBRARY AND ARCHIVES CANADA CATALOGUING IN PUBLICATION

Title: None of this belongs to me / Ellie Sawatzky.
Names: Sawatzky, Ellie, 1990- author.
Description: Poems.
Identifiers: Canadiana (print) 20210245352 | Canadiana (ebook) 20210245360 | ISBN 9780889714083 (softcover) | ISBN 9780889714090 (HTML)
Classification: LCC PS8637.A9265 N66 2021 | DDC C811/.6—dc23

be soaked unloading the car. Our minds will go.
The horizon is another colour we know.

LOOK AT YOUR LIFE YOU'LL SEE EMILYS

Emilys in ice skates casting circles on the lake

skipping Sunday school for kittens uttering

tampon and *bra* like *pencil* while you still

swallow the words Emilys make molehills

of snowbanks jump in juniper offer goat's milk

cocoa heather smoke and breath fog yawning

on the boardwalk Emilys at eighteen hold

your hair hold your hand through cemeteries

piercings when your father is sick some Emilys

drive Civics some Emilys are Emilee and little

or they're tall scald their throats with whisky

get excited settle down some Emilys incite

poetry festivals impersonate Alanis teach dance

as magic expression shaking hurt from their hips

so many Emilys—or Emilies—plucky

millennials shifting wild-minded they rock climb

sew costumes for their cross-dressing husbands

tend the land black-handed in marsh boots

Emilys cry on Skype Emilys bus tables insert

IUDs feed geese forget to eat Emilys hunt ghosts

shovel snow get nervous in crowds quietly

paint highland cows Emilys casting circles

Emilys amassing gifting apples to a fire

FINLANDIA

Two shots of Patrón as I leave
for Lisa's Mormon family
Christmas party. In her pink

kitchen, I drink root beer,
eat Amish fruitcake, and meet
her new husband,

a missionary. Married
over the summer
in Joseph Smith's white

phallus. I've been scared
to see her since the wedding,
afraid to find her pious,

wifely. But she's the same
sweet girl in granny glasses.
A family friend leans across

the granite countertop,
tells me his opinion of
"the homosexual situation."

My hot palms, tequila-scented
sweat. Lisa, in the corner,
opens the black casket

of our friendship. The sad
sour smell of mildewed velour,
neglected brass, musk

of a high school music room.
Those days we watched our faces thin
and fatten in our trombones'

yellow metal, playing "Take Five"
and "Fly Me to the Moon."
Now, "Finlandia,"

a song from an old workbook.
"It's really a hymn,"
her dad says, "Be Still My Soul."

"Finlandia," Lisa says, and we play
slowly, badly, dumbing
down to the same

off-key. We've always found
this neutral ground, never
speaking of God. Collecting

freckle pelt and treeflute lichen
for fairies, a stick and a rock
for a unicorn skull. We both believed

in tulip bulbs, guerrilla
gardening on our high school's
front lawn. And trombone—

its potential to weep
or bellow. When the song
ends, we pull back,

smiling, touching
our swollen mouths. Shy,
as if we'd been kissing.

THE BOY NEXT DOOR

As kids, we tried to sell rocks to the cottagers.
Pink granite, red shale, gypsum. Bouquets
of dandelion and stinkweed at a reasonable price.
Sand, lake scum, crayfish in plastic buckets.
I showed him the little mound where we buried
my drowned hedgehog. We rode our bikes
to the bait shop for candy, found
an abandoned playhouse in the woods,
its mouldy stuffed animals, eyes still bright.

Winter, we shovelled snow into a pile,
built a quinzhee on the frozen lake. Crawled
in and out of it, playing *I'm the king of the ice cave,*
guess who's the dirty ice slave until the sky bruised
and I could see a patch of stars between his knees.

Inside, we lit candles, cut shelves in the walls
to hold them. A glow in the glistening blue-white.
Fruity steam of his breath, the smell of his boy sweat
like rubber, dry leaves. A shake of greenish freckles
on his nose. Cold salt of his lips, warm hollow
of his mouth. The comfortless crush of our snowsuits
when I leaned into him, the surprise in his eyes,
wet lashes like new wings.
                              I gotta go home.

After that I saw him less. And less,
and then years later heard he was the one
to find his father dead, heart burst
in his chest. Summer, the fan still blowing
and pieces of the man's hair lifting
like feathers on a roadside crow.

Later still, his mother's car skidded
on the black-iced highway, taking out the guardrail
like it was made of pipe cleaner.
When he saw her face in the hospital, pale,
smiling, he wanted to smack her for acting
like it was no big deal, and the doctor
for saying she was lucky to be alive.
They didn't know his world had run after her,
like a dog into that ravine below Sioux Narrows,
where it trembled and looked and with nowhere left
to go, circled once round her warped car, and slept.

The neighbours still like to talk about it.
The way he lost control—breaking
into every house in our woods, broad daylight.
Drugs, drinking. *Pornography*, like the wickedest
of all sins, they whisper, *pornography*.

His face—the day I caught him skulking outside
our garage—blank and cool as a glass of water.
He said my name, hands deep
in his pockets. Moved closer.

                    Can I borrow a cup of sugar?

And now his own mother doesn't know
where he got to, what form of shelter
he finds at night.

To think I see him cross the frozen water,
the white lip of the shoreline curved, pleased
at his return. A boy in a snowsuit with a shovel,
just kissed. And uphill, the copper smell
of earth under snow. He goes into
the lit house.

RECALCULATING

I'm twenty-four and this is not a first. Dad
in the driver's seat, Mom in charge

of map and unflappable GPS voice.
I lean on the warm west window.

Are we there yet? and *How
long?* and *I have to pee* an hour

out of Portland, seeing my life
in reverse. Cows in the fields shrink

to calves, barn wood rehydrates. We stop
at every brewery for Brown Nectar,

Dead Guy Ale. Dad's not allowed
to practise medicine since his stroke, so at sixty

he seeks a career—he'll farm cranberries
or restore Westfalia vans, open

a gastropub, a gentlemen's shop
that sells belts. A move to Spain

or Mendocino. He asks Mom
if a bakery would fly in Belize. She says

it depends on the flour. I offer raspberries,
cold from the zipperless cooler.

Too quiet, so I Bluetooth Tom Petty,
talk and sing 'til someone snaps

me shut. In the silence now
we're all adults and no one knows

what's best. Dusk greens the highway.
At a Days Inn by the ocean, we slip out

of our glasses, click bedside lamps.
The three of us blink in the black room

like mice. Sea lions bark orders all night.

I PRESS AN EAR TO ONTARIO

In Jack's Pub, Tofino,
a local man holds my hand,

tells me he was born
in Kenora. His mother

hurled him in tea-coloured
Lake of the Woods when he

was less than three
weeks old. *'Course I survived,*

can't you see me?
Grey hair stiff with salt,

eyes that swim in tannin
pools. He still goes back, calls it

home, like I do. Where freshwater
licks the slate shoreline.

Outside, the tide
rises, ocean flickering

like TV static. I press an ear
to Ontario. My mother's

voice in the smooth tunnel
of the telephone. She's alone

in the loft with her nine-patch
and oldies channel. Hopeful

quilts on every wall, and Lassie
bounding black and white

across the Scottish Highlands.

CHIHULY'S MILLE FIORI

In the dark gallery we look at the glass.
Grasses, snakes. Bulrushes and flushes of colour.
My sister and I—we're charcoal-supple, still calm;
it's a full moon tonight, and later we'll go dancing.

Grasses and snakes. Bulrushes, flushes of colour,
while Dad's on a stretcher waiting for a brain scan.
It's a full moon tonight, and later we'll go dancing.
We look at the glass. One thousand flowers.

And Dad's on a stretcher waiting for a brain scan.
Somewhere else, a different city. Everything feels right.
We look at the glass. One thousand flowers
reflected in a black pool, drowsy.

Somewhere else, a different city. Nothing feels right.
In the hospital it's never dark. Fluorescent moons
reflect in the black windows, manless.
And we don't know yet what's happened.

In the hospital it's never dark. Fluorescent moons
in the windows, flashes of white like fractured bone.
We don't know yet what's happened.
Innocent minutes drift between the glass cattails.

The windows, flashes of white like fractured bone.
My sister and I—we're charcoal-supple, so calm.
Innocent minutes drift between the stalks of cattails.
We sit in the dark garden. Look at the beautiful glass.

II

POETRY WANTS MY IMAGINARY BOYFRIENDS

one human voice
amid such choruses of desire

—Lucille Clifton

TOM PETTY SAID LOVE IS A LONG ROAD BUT I THINK LOVE IS A CIRCLE

I open my memory and out comes a castle

I unlock the castle

and out comes a kiss

I question the kiss and out comes a stranger

I pester the stranger

and out comes some yarn I untangle the yarn and out

come your fingers I unfasten your fingers and

out comes an anger I press on the anger

and out comes a prayer

I recount the prayer and out comes a lake

I trouble the lake and out comes the winter

I confess things to winter and out comes a wanting

brush snow from the wanting and out comes a song

I sing along and out comes my memory

I open my memory

my memory unrolls

POETRY WANTS MY IMAGINARY BOYFRIENDS

Truth rambles some moorish in-between,
but that's poetry. Poetry wants

Obsidian, Pierrot, Lyon. Grade nine.
I called myself
Oak Tree. Insufferable.

With my first flesh and blood boyfriend,
confused by the blocky
awkwardness of love. A mix

of tenderness and blueberry vodka—his dad's
house on the lake, hot-boxed
bathroom. Bed upstairs where I ditched
the social construct of virginity listening
to Radiohead.

Should have left it behind
the percussion instruments in the music room,
timpani slowly untuning,
or better yet, to the girl painting murals
in the next town over.

Should have sabotaged
every relationship, touched magic, moonrise,
travelled to Barcelona and gotten laid. Or
I should still be a virgin.

Poetry wants my awkwardness
and smooth slip into promiscuity,
wants me to malfunction
perfectly forever. Lucky

this splitting pain is in the name
of something, lucky
poetry wants my ache and ache and a thumb
lost to frostbite. Poetry wants to shake

things up, break it off, cut my hair.
Sell my eggs so I might have
children in the world—mine,

not mine at the same time. Poetry
wants those children to find me.

IF YOU'RE WRITING THIS DOWN

i. winter

we have to only say nice things Grandma says

falling asleep on the couch squash
crackling in the oven I dream abt animals
running thru the bush

Grandma says *no one knows*
why we're here

ritual ablutions whisky

in my childhood bedroom I find a cheque
I never cashed 40 bucks
from the bookstore in Kenora folded
between the pages of a paperback romance *Suddenly*
You first idea of money first of sex

the last thing I Googled was *Mennonite women sexuality*

at Auntie Wendy's house
art on the wall says
you haven't had a night until you've had
a Mennonite

Tinder profile?

Grandma says *you can't help but feel free*

the guy next to me on the plane
tells me to visit whopayswriters.com

is freedom the opposite of anxiety?

what's the opposite of stone?

ii. spring

the man I love is somewhere thinking
about pyramids and old rocks   how the earth
might be flat

conspiracy   conspire   breathe with
go along with   thus to follow an idea
into eternity/black hole

I buy a globe for $6 at the Salvation Army
bc fuck that

you can't help but feel free

the words for sewing wax and sex are next
to each other in the Plautdietsch dictionary   there are
seven different words for pigpen

Auntie Sandy says Great-Grandpa Schellenberg
had a moonshine still

Mom sends me pictures of our ancestors
being exhumed when the farm sold   skull
and lace collar

Grandma says   *all these stories sound a little other but*

I write down   *wedding dress reused*

iii. summer

> people from her time never admit anything
> went wrong—*20th Century Women*

last night I slept better bc a deer slept
outside my window

airport bathrooms never not playing Shakira

halved plums like blue hearts
inside perogies (Grandma taught me)

the last thing I Googled was *watch project free tv*

the only phrase I remember in Plautdietsch
means *mind your own business* (Grandma taught me)

no one knows why we're here

iv. fall

I use the ferry Wi-Fi to watch
ASMR roleplays   stare at the sea
and have my eyebrows shaped by a woman
on the Internet with a hard
American accent   acrylic nails
her baby's footprint tattooed on her neck

the ferry doors open like an opera

on the island I try to feel free

what's the opposite of island?

we hike thru mountain shadow
giant rhubarb   tiny ferns that look
like insect skeletons

if the earth is flat   I ask him   *then what
does it look like?*

v. winter

watching *Under the Tuscan Sun*
and masturbating = freedom

or that time Grandma helped out the Hells Angels

it's a kind of happiness   this sadness

cloudy   the sun looks like the moon
from the airplane   the country's a slow read

falling asleep on Grandma's couch   I dream
I'm an animal running thru the bush
to get here

RHINOCEROTIC

All night, they feed outside
our cabin, hog-shuffling
between silver oaks,
fever trees. Hooved feet
in shortgrass, tearing
the earth. I crouch
in the doorway, watching.
Remember to breathe,
come back to my own
rough body. Scarred
teenaged skin, breasts
that rose in the dark.
Sixteen, muggy
with hormones. Drunk
on antimalarials and lack
of sleep. The night moves,
greenish and muscled,
and me with it, far
from home, from my strange,
young boyfriend. I want
to tell him I'm ready.
To press into something,
to bite and break the skin.
To drink the juice of a moon
full to bursting, before it thins
to a sun-bleached rib.
All night, the dark lines
of rhinos. In the cabin,
the pulsing ultrasound
of a gecko inside a lampshade.

FORGIVE US OUR TRESPASSES

A girl lies & says the cat belongs to her.

A girl is mean to the girl who eats ChapStick.

A girl keeps a deer tick in a jar.

A girl refuses to unbraid & that girl gets her head shaved.

A girl lives in Normal.

A girl lives in Hexville.

A girl cleans period blood off the couch.

A girl doesn't feel like a girl but wishes to be a sister.

A girl is a babysitter.

A girl is a waitress who spends her quiet hours dusting driftwood.

A girl likes when the music is loud & buzzes in her lap.

A girl feels old, confuses gingersnaps with snapshots.

A girl feels like twelve geese inside a person costume.

A girl sees a man pee her name in the sand.

A girl lets a man sing hymns to her in a windstorm.

A girl lets a man enter her tent.

The first girl just wants something to belong to her

& so she follows the cat into the ravine.

SUMMER WORK

Morning, all sweat and hay, sky
smoke-grey, blind, blue-eyed collie
at my heel. Earwigs
in the bottom of the wheelbarrow.

I catch your eye across the yard, the tilt
of your shoulders, hitching Carhartts
on skinny hips. One
unsteady moment, a tree pressed forward
in a windstorm, then back
and on your way, hammer swinging
from your hand.

In the barn, the white goat
begins to bellow.

Minutes run like mice along the moss-
soaked eaves, blood and slime in webs
across the straw. The white goat
with gasping sides tries to stand.

Tangled mess of birth, the first
I've seen. It leaves me dry, empty,
tasting my teeth.

You take my hand, pull me sideways
into the abandoned ice cream stand
in the woods. Tack a rag
to the service window, eat
the afternoon in hungry spoonfuls
and when there's nothing left, lie
in silence, twigs cracking, raccoons
on the roof.

Evening, leather stink of livestock,
ocean musk through the poplars.
A charcoal smudge of a heron
against the sky.

The babies are pink-kneed,
milk-bellied, bawling long vowels
in the fading light.

You start away across the yard and every
goat turns her head.

CAMELS IN THE CARIBOO

I come back
as a camel. Adapt

to rainshadow
and softly stirring

firs. 1862, my ancestors
bow-legged in the low

belly of a ship, humps
of wilted leather. Blinded

by a still moonlit
morning in Lillooet,

sent mewling up
the hill. A few months,

maybe, 'til history
gets vicious, turned

loose. Century later,
I'm the living memory

of Gold Rush soap
eaters, eastern

silhouette against
the colourless Cariboo

sunrise. This time
I've got freedom

bred into me. I never
have to see another

human. River drinker,
shadow flinger, deep

in the valleys where
the right story rings.

THREE DAYS AND THE NEXT HOWEVER LONG

In the dark, we scramble eggs. Lucie's blue-lit kitchen,
maple syrup to sweeten coffee, breakfast tea,
loaves of homemade bread still soft and sweating.

Fireflies in the fields between Lennoxville
and Cookshire, the shopworn sign:
Ferme Paysanne: Oeufs frais, Poulet, Porc.
Taylor and I bunch in the back seat of Lucie's jeep with stacks
of cardboard crates, their rows of portholes for two thousand Cochin
chicks, still damp. We set them loose

among the coop's pine-sweet shavings, sweating in the close,
copper heat, teach them to drink from nozzles along
a length of pipe. One death, the body crumpled,
purple lids squeezed shut. Lucie says it happens.

The next day, two thousand motherless birds
and sixteen dead, pecked bloody. A parasite,
Lucie says, or some sickness carried in
on our skin, our boots. She talks minerals, electrolytes
and I want to believe she knows best.

Taylor and I refuse eggs, the leftover chicken.
At Restaurant 108 across the highway,
we drink Cariboo on a terrace, breathing woodsmoke,
storm clouds, dung. Tins of tuna from the truck stop feed
stray cats circling the barn.

When we wake, one hundred dead and counting. The air
sour, shavings slick with shit. We collect bodies in white plastic buckets,
separating the dead from the not-yet-dead from the living.
It goes on. At five o'clock, Lucie leaves to make dinner,
then Taylor, red-faced, worn out.

Alone, patron saint of poultry, I build stations.
I don't get tired or hungry, checking for heartbeats.
I carry the dead in buckets.

Outside, the air is mineral, metallic, the smell
rain shares with blood. Water runs in thick veins
through Lucie's garden, batters the barn roof.
In the dark, I rinse my boots.
The water pools, sinks, and moves on.

SUN VALLEY LODGE

Somewhere in my mind, you've become
inseparable from the old boats, the plastic
Adirondack chairs. Listen, I saw plastic
Adirondack chairs long before I ever
saw you. I also saw red cars, fireweed,
deer in the road. I saw ukuleles and *Amélie*.
I rolled my own cigarettes, smoked them
alone, I crocheted poems to keep warm
at night before you, so step back, love,
this is my line of pine trees. This is my
soft light falling fast behind the lake.

HIPPOCRENE

after John Steffler

Late July outside St. Isidore, summer heat
creaking in the apple trees. Following the path
to our tent—silver slug-eye glint of wet gravel,
wind in grass and leaves, hills, trees,
wilted during the day by heat and hangover,
back to shaking shaggy backsides while thunder
thumped and strobe lightning outlined the barn ahead,
a DJ in a farmyard nightclub—some

bit of brightness separated from the rest and leapt
towards us, maybe a preening posse of snowy owls, maybe a
Great Dane with a hairdo, it was a

filly, wild child, free from sleep, weird
with electricity. She charged out of the night buzzing
and tripping, lines and stars, a fine
piece of sky. We tried

to back away—graceless, stiff—but she
pranced circles around us in platform heels.

She was the wheel of a wagon rolling loose, she struck
us down.

She was a musical ride escaped from the travelling
fair of our childhoods. She
remembered us.

She coursed and sputtered.
Her eyes were like eyes watching whirlpools,
like blossoms blossoming. Like elevator doors
opening to the four hundred and forty-fourth floor.

She was warm, thunderstorm-scented, she nudged us
like we were trees.

She made us wish we were dust on the smooth
fabric of her stomach, she made us sweat.

She made us stutter. She was a cage full of fight.

A willow of a girl in a white dress. Shy,
we whispered *enchanté*, offered our hands.

She could have cantered across the country.
She was headstrong relative of rhino. Still, she'd been
lured by apples, bluegrass. Sold her soft
body for room and board.

She was renamed by Jacques Cartier. Claimed
and claimed.

Men had tried to tame her. Horse goddess, she'd worn
a gold bridle and sipped from a bucket. Paced
behind an electric line.

Now, stripped bare.

A piece of the province, rivers
connecting lung-and-liver-shaped lakes.

THE MISSED CONNECTIONS AD WRITES ITSELF

I'm still thinking
about the beautiful man
who sweetly asked me out
outside the New Apple Farm Market
where I was feeding B strawberries
from a paper carton. She was four
or five, blonde enough to be my daughter,
offering strawberry stems to her small
blind dog. I startled
at his question and fumbled to explain
I was not mother to this child
or this dog, but nevertheless
unavailable for a date and
we parted ways, both of us confused
and at least one of us a bit awestruck
by the tiny awkward love poem
that had just fluttered open
on the sidewalk.

OUROBOROS

Roadside, the white car
idles. B doesn't know

she won't always be a child,
the way I didn't know I'd be

thrust into this thistle-stitched
ditch of adulthood.

My twenty-six years to
her three. She squats behind

sagebrush. I hover nearby
in a beige patch of shade,

blending in with the
frumpy umbrella trees.

Hours in the back seat
reading books about witches,

horses, finches, pink
illustrations of karma

and friendship—the last
hour of which she refused

to sit. Her mother, ouroboros
tattoo and alligator shoe on

the gas, cursing signboards,
the forecast, her lack of

control. She didn't know
she'd feel old. Now,

she paces the shoulder while
I chase B weakly through

milkweed. The heat, the days
catching up to me. The desert's

cyclical imagery. Smoke,
creosote, crows nosing dark

piles of roadkill. The desert
for miles. A fresh start

digressing in the rattler-happy
crabgrass, a stick to flip

over this fear.

NOUNOU

I sit with B in her kitchen, discuss
a Safeway bouquet
of lilies. I say *lis*. B says

maman accidentally.

None of this belongs
to me. B cradles a plastic baby.

I think of the girl on the box
of Borax with a girl on it holding
a box of Borax.

I feel like Pluto, my planethood

questioned. The mess
of identity. I am most like

my lover when I question
the moon landing.

I am most like my mother when I say
bougainvillea, book

flights. Most like B in my need.

She's terrified, B says, squeezing
her baby. *Terrified means
beautiful in French.*

Once, *sea, Pomeranian, mother,*
nanny were just

colours she'd learn
to compare. Now she sits

at an IKEA dining table,
testing new waters for fear,
beauty, lilies. Evening,

the neighbour's cat streaks in,
cold, reeking of rosemary.

B folds in sleep, a flare
of lily dust up her sleeve.

She won't remember

how I carried her past
train-track blackberries, backyard
chickens. The summer

BC burned and ferns stirred
the earth.

She was born, tasted sweat, dog fur,
swam in the sea.

COWHIDE, PLASTIC

When I was a child, I tried to make sense
of a bust, clay breasts above

my parents' bed. In my mother's closet,
scents of incense, old silk. The dusty animal

of her life brushing past to the places she went
without me. Tonight,

rain taps patio windows. Rustle of rats
in the geraniums. Three a.m. in a house, not mine,

a child asleep upstairs, one-eyed
Pomeranian bumping blindly round

my ankles. On the bookshelf,
The Holy Bible elbows *S&M Feminist,*

The Complete Shakespeare Sonnets.
How did I grow up and arrive

here, of all places, and who are
these people with their cowhide

from Key West, Pomeranian peeing
in the corner on plastic grass. Grown-ups

made me, explained things like sex
and art and garbage. Lately I've been

explaining. Clay is mouldable earth,
cowhide and plastic mean death. Death:

predestined. Poetry: the way the night
tries to make sense of its day,

rat-coloured, rustling pages.

SHIBARI

(for B)

Your mother wants
to practise—and who better
than me? We leave you

at preschool, take the highway.
Sky fading to Burnaby
grey. D-u-n-g-e-o-n,

a suburban basement where I
drink Sprite, study a wall of
sex spatulas. Your mother

shows me the ropes. She jokes
about her dominatrix days in LA,
loops lavender jute around

my legs. I once went
to an art party where
a woman cocooned

in plastic wrap was meant
to rip herself free. But
for a while she just

swung there, and now
I understand. The burden
of my body lifted from me

briefly, winched
skyward. I see myself
tied up from the other

side of the room, and I feel
light. Kinbaku, *the beauty
of tight binding.* Your mother—

mistress, artist—naming knots.
*Lark's head. Half-hitch.
This is kimono.* This

is prayer. Rope drunk,
we're late to pick you up.
You in the glare of falling

daylight. Your clamour,
your brilliant demands. You reach
for me, pull me, and I puppet

for you. I stare soberly at the road
going home, try to remember
kimono, prayer. Ties,

coming loose.

THIS LITTLE GIRL GOES TO BURNING MAN

> *A Leave No Trace Ethic is very simple: leave the place you visit the*
> *same as or better than you found it.*
> —Burning Man Guide

This little girl is one-two-three. We count mountain goats from the RV
window, the spread-open wings of dragon trees,
and brittle blue shrubs
as they dwindle

to *one over there* and then none. Under paper-white sky, it's *Tutu Tuesday*,
it's a Day-Glo desert playground, she's
a dust fairy in pink
half-blinking,

never sits. Me, her nanny, mistaken for her mother. She's had less time
than some to learn the horselike unpredictability
of love. Her mother
runs free

in beaded boots, a faux-fur bikini. Repeating *love*, her mantra, the word
sounding in the black mountain valley,
or swallowed whole, a bell
in a mossy

hollow. This mother was three, then forty-three in a flare of wildfire. She
was a little girl wanting love. Her own mother
loved the dog, and a man
who ran

marathons. This little girl wants to see the man burn. Long into the black,
ecstatic night, she's lighting matches, while I
lie awake in limbo. Listening
to little huffs

of breath, the threat of hooves outside, stirring up dust storms, the sound
nearly drowned by drumfunk, thumping
bass. This little girl's out dancing,
this little girl's

asleep. This little girl, with turning uncertainty, loves another little girl,
and the love leaves its trace,
lit up like a glowstick,
then slowly

leaking esters into sand.

CRYSTALS

B clicks fistfuls of amethysts. B is six. Earlier this week,
in an Agassiz campground, she held a tiny
abandoned rabbit. *Watership Down*,
but with ravers,

fire driving out the wildlife for the new wild life, EDM
and bike lights, B's mother gripping
capsules stuffed
with crystals

in her fist. I tell my mother I never want kids. My mother teaches
motherhood in Ontario woods, leads La Leche League,
squirrels worn-out clothes
for quilts to send

overseas. My blood is hot, monthly, laced with misanthropy.
These years as B's nanny, her nature scraping
against my nurture.
Her mother

couldn't breastfeed, couldn't risk trickling helixes of infected
T cells, says she sometimes senses this
distance. What bits of
my mother

insist in me? To what do I affix our distance? The burr thicket of it,
sticky. The body's crystal arithmetic. B gives me
an amethyst, tells me how
the rabbit's heart

beat beneath her fingertips.

SWAN SONG

I thought we were out of each other's
lives for good but here you are
in my Facebook inbox,
your nine-year-old eyes behind
a goth princess filter.

> *hey what's up*
> *guess what this is a drawing of.*

A hat? Or a hockey net.

The part of me that still worries
about you clicks on like a noisy TV.
Your wicked face, my first day. You
not even one yet, wheeling
out of your mom's bedroom, trailing
her snake whip. Out on the street
you warped away from me, quick
as a quarter horse.

I don't remember the first time
you reached for me.

What did you do today?

> *I went to cooking it was so fun*
> *and I had my movie so I guess*
> *I'll see all the hearts.*

A cold sweet surreality,
texting with you while I pretend
to pay attention to my Zoom meeting.
Carrying you in my pocket as I carry someone
else's baby down your street.

Late August leaves brindle
against a dull grey sky. I remember
when you offered me relationship advice:
You should try to agree on something.
I remember when you asked me
how my writing was going. You were three.

I don't remember the last time
I saw you. Was it tea at your place?
Your mom chattering about the scene
she'd booked on a TV show,
how she'd been rehearsing
her tortured scream. Or maybe
it was outside the sushi restaurant.
You didn't see me. You were in
a red coat, turning away, your hand
in your new nanny's.

> *I can't speak your hair can be*
> *very sunny today sorry I am*
> *the voice thing jump on at my words.*

You are new to this kind of (dis)
connection. You'll discover GIF hugs
and cartoon emotions. Maybe
you already know, have amassed
coloured hearts in a little
glowing bowl on your nightstand,
exercised a broken one.

　　　Guess what this is a drawing of.

The spine of a book? Shirtsleeve?
A fallen birch tree? Or a bridge
growing lonesome
between us. Took me a minute.
But now I see it.

MATRILINEAL

My soul doth magnify the Lord.
And my spirit hath rejoiced in God my Saviour.
For he hath regarded: the lowliness of his handmaiden: For
behold, from henceforth: all generations shall call me blessed.
—Mary's Song of Praise: The Magnificat, Luke 1:46–55

In this Coal Harbour café the barista plays
her baby's fetal heartbeat over

the sound system. I coax the stroller
into a corner table, fold a blanket under the petals

of the sleeping baby's ears. Out the window
I can see a cook from Cardero's having a cigarette

on the seawall. Same guy who once grabbed my arm
as I passed, asked if I had a husband.

On the corner, a woman sells bananas
from a plastic bag. A man floats by with a bouquet

of greyhounds. Each of us, our daily intermittent
bursts of purpose. I rifle through the messy purse

that is my heart, offbeat with the swishing speakers.
Find Mary, great-grandmother, named for the Mother,

but not hers, Helena, who died of milk fever
one month after the birth of her twentieth child.

I see Mary at twelve, on a footbridge
praying to Jesus. A merganser wallows

in the swamp beneath her, lifts off suddenly.
Someone once told Mary, like someone

once told me, that the screams of grasshoppers
come from between the knees.

The barista beams, tearful, at me and the sleeping baby
she doesn't know is not my baby

while she pulls my espresso. Around us, the speakers
pulse eerily. She has just told her co-workers

she's pregnant. I think of the pink plastic test
in my purse. *Congratulations,* I say,

sweating sharp stars through the AC.
I seep through my mother's dress.

Many ways to be named *mother*, to claim space.
Mary's older siblings marry,

move away. The rest of the family settles
and unsettles abandoned Manitoba farmhouses

built by Mennonite refugee ancestors in a drowned
land. At night, Mary lies awake. Frogs creak

like hinges. Stormlight radiates across her baby sisters'
faces. Their father comes home late, brimming

with whisky. Mary, silent, pours his coffee, tucks
him in, slips out into the wet knit of night

to unhitch the horse from its buggy. In the Bible,
Mary sings, *For he that is mighty hath magnified me.*

I double tap mechanically on Instagram.
Engagement, job announcement,

ultrasound video shivering
with static. Mary greyscale in a garden.

These days I don't know what's me, what's
inherited, a dream, the Internet.

As the eldest girl, Mary is too busy mothering
her siblings to go to school, never learns

how to read. Sisters paddle marshlands of stories
with their eyes. Mary sews clothes from kitchen rags,

grasps together loaves of bread with handfuls
of clay loam. Molasses sandwiches, boiled bones.

My mother texts me her dream: warblers for ears—
her children—then they are just her ears.

How's baby? I say he'll sleep another hour, maybe,
then I'll bring him home to his mother.

Google: *Plautdietsch word for pregnant.*
If a ghost is after life then what's

a fetus? What is its possibility? Pre-life,
it settles among us, unsettles and shimmers

unseen. My mother always knew she wanted
children. My sister dreams nightly of bright

canola fields and sweet blonde babies.
Our church basement childhood—*zwieback* and *paska*,

sour coffee, songs like "Johnny Appleseed"
and "Jesus Loves Me" thick in our teeth.

And holy is his Name, sings Mary,
or does she? I click through Wikipedia,

skim *scholarly discussion*, then: *Luke portrays her
as the singer of this song.* Mary as happy bolster

to a timber-frame story. Humbled
by the weight of responsibility, incandescent

over a surprise pregnancy. Sure.
Or maybe she was more like me. The word

Kjaakjsche ghosts my tongue. *To witness.
To be female. To serve.* As a nanny,

I weave in and out of tradition. In this café,
in this city two thousand miles from Mary, I'm steeped

in other people's spirits. Last week,
baby's grandmother visited from Cambodia

and the air in the apartment teemed, breathy.
In the future, will he attempt to seize the wisps

of his history? What kind of man will he rise up
to be? Rain flicks at the window. When I look,

baby's looking too. My mother texts: *I'm going for a swim*
while the bread rises. In case you try to call.

He hath filled the hungry with good things,
Mary supposedly sings.

At fifteen, my great-grandmother Mary
goes to work as a *Kjaakjsche*—scullion, nanny

for another motherless family. Another word
for widower—harrow, hunger. Girl

a flash of blue mistaken for a woman.
And his mercy is on them that fear him.

What the body needs. What it means
when he says, *De Mana oabeide enn*

de Frues hiele. Men work and women weep.
Mary in the kitchen baking *zwieback*—the larger bun

holding the smaller on its shoulders.
Mary weeping. Mary bleeding.

Google: *Muttaschkaunt. Muttasproak.*
To feed. To bleed into. To bring

into being. *As it was in the beginning, is now,*
and ever shall be. Mary, nineteen when she marries,

Mary on a footbridge praying to Jesus.
Mourning doves grieve in switchgrass. Mary,

can you already see yourself growing rows
of daughters in a tidied plot? Teaching them

to bake bread with real flour and flax and then
dying quietly? To rise up in silence from the dirt, everything

rising. Balloons we released at your graveside
when I was six, my only memory.

I take the test in the café bathroom, stroller
on the other side of the stall. Not *schwoafallijch,*

just late. Not haunted by one date with a man
who plays teenagers in Netflix movies.

Awash in choice, it climbs the sides of me.
The future is as it always was, a quivering

night lit occasionally by lightning. *World*
without end. In the illumined instants: A girl

unhitching a horse from its buggy. A girl
asleep. A girl in the frame of a window, reading.

The baby grasps at my dress,
which was my mother's dress, hungry.

This is not a tidy story. It's possible
I hoped Mary would make a home

of this poem, this body. Far from the prairies,
I grasp at her like I expect her to feed me.

Like she hasn't already. Many reasons
women weep. My mother texts: *How are you?*

and I don't know what to say.
Grey skirts of rain hike up over Coal Harbour.

Baby waves goodbye to the barista
who is still crying happily.

The ghost of the ocean creeps, salty,
between us, through the strange familiar minutes

we all pass through eventually. On the seawall,
I pray to a disorganized sky

my great-grandmother Mary called Jesus.
Ask for nothing. Offer thanks.

IV

UNORGANIZED TERRITORY

You won't want to sleep. But staying up
so late won't teach you anything. Better
to look in a dream. That's the way in to
leaving.

—Gemini Horoscope, Astro Poets tweet

GOODBYE

after "The Coup" by Patricia Piccinini

Tableau: a silicone-and-fibreglass boy
with a taxidermal parrot on his arm, his features
simian, the hotel room destroyed, one hand poised

to strike or stroke the bird, we'll never know.
I've been categorizing good and bad lately
for the little boy I nanny who, last week, lobbed

a monster truck at the TV, smashed the screen.
He looked at me, triumphant, he'd made something happen.
When he reaches for his baby brother

we all suck air through our teeth. Will he be good
or bad, this tiny revolutionary, how many times
will he hurt or be hurt, shall we

start the tally? It's hard to love
in this backstage manner. I'll be relieved
to leave, the way I was at my last job,

the way I was when I left the hotel tonight,
the boy with the parrot behind me
in a bright room, his outstretched hand landing softly.

NEW MOON, GEMINI SEASON

Someone on Instagram said
    you can begin again

Across the city the man I used to love
    is happy likely

waxing metaphysical to his cats
    about the Illuminati

I'm feverish in bed the Internet feeding me
    little wisdoms I don't believe

in romance a friend says in a text
    and I protest

but these days an ASMRtist on YouTube
    pets me to sleep

The little boy I nanny says he sees ghosts
    I guess I believe

in unfinished business like when the Big One
    shakes us I imagine I'll be high

on cough syrup rolling bad nineties movies
    in my mind and wishing

I could call my mother but lately
    I just ask Google

at least I know I'm not the first person
　　to have wondered

anything wikiHow can I begin again
　　if I'm still haunted how

do I make peace with my ex
　　who believed

the Flat Earth Theory fell asleep each night
　　listening to lectures

by a man known as Mr. Astrotheology
　　I hated that NASA loomed

monstrous outside our house
　　that even love

might have been a conspiracy
　　We circled each other

for so many years I saw my Saturn
　　returning and a so-called

antimoon finally shadowed
　　him from me

I'm wide awake now even in sleep
　　I'm busy building catastrophes

Last night's nightmare a gym floor
　　littered with thumbtacks

many barefoot children
        But hope

this evening is a post-Tinder codeine dream
        where I see two of me

make love to each other while
        the earth quakes

I believe this is the beginning
        of something

BLESSINGS UPON U AND UR BULLSHIT

for my neighbour

but also fuck u
the yoga's not working
and i hate u and ur audi q7
which before today
before i knew what kind
of woman handled her
i thought was kinda beautiful
actually
i could maybe feel a bit sorry
for the audi
poor elephant
it's not her fault
but u who threatened
to have my car towed
bc it was parked in front of
ur house
u who own the street u
epithet of imperialist
white capitalist
heteronormativity
u said
u'll understand when ur
a mom u said
u'll understand
when ur a homeowner
but i won't
i will never be like u
bad girl
my landlady said to me

when i told her
bad girl stop barking
at the neighbours
and all night
she walked over me
i pay her
so she owns me
u own me too apparently
and u bought ur human costume
at banana republic
so it doesn't matter
that u barked first
and louder
i wish some bad stuff for u
like an infestation of
immortal mice
that bustle under the covers
and all over u
while ur sleeping
and when u call the exterminator
she says she doesn't deal
in the immortal mouse variety
even when u say
don't u know who i am
there's no point
u have to just give in to it
ur powerless against the mice
like im powerless against u
except im not
i know this
i lie down
not bc u told me to
but bc there is no such thing

as an immortal mouse
and bc i know
im lucky
down here so close
to the earth
i can feel it

WAYS TO WRITE A POEM

Imagine how you might be murdered, but
make it beautiful.

Think about sex but never do it.

Unlearn how to swim.

List eleven hundred verbs
and types of trees.

Think about which of your friends you'd
have sex with and why.

Say everything you might want to say
to your ex, but you're a bird.

Sit in a room with some
blank-faced balloons until
you burst.

Don't drink anything, not even
coffee. Be thirsty.

Imagine you're in a car full of poets
and the car explodes, but
add magic.

Cut off a single finger.

Put on black lipstick.

Touch the white part
of the fire.

UNTITLED

for Erin Kirsh & Reece Cochrane

These days, we walk because it beats taking
the bus. Cruise Craigslist, brainstorm names for future
bicycles. We feel brilliant at night in not-quite

rain when we've been invited to art parties
with free brie and tiny cakes at places
called Pipe Shop or Shipyards, fucked

by morning when we wake in our basements,
the effects of white wine hurting at the hairline,
world maps curling damply off the walls.

These days, we keep our windows open, hoping
for cats. We walk until our shins splint. Our mothers
tell us this is good, because exercise is just

as effective as Xanax. Our mothers
tell us there are people who've lost hands
who still play piano, so we should be more

positive. We take care of our houseplants,
give them names like K'naan, Alanis, Carly Rae.
Some days, we feel better than okay.

We host clothing swaps, trade sex
for tickets to Shakespeare plays, house-sit
for Chardonnay, exchange for fiddle lessons

exchange for massages or pot or over-the-sink
haircuts or life advice or tampons or childcare
for our landlords' cable so we can watch

The Bachelorette Canada while smelling
our borrowed cats for comfort. We splurge
on pine nuts, bright lipstick, sandals handmade

in California, tickets to see bands
whose Latin-inspired trumpet solos sound
out over English Bay, and we consider

again the possibility that this is better than okay.
These days, I swear the wet sidewalks smell
sweeter when you're only a few steps away.

KNIFE THROWER

Of course he's the first
after you. He's questions I don't

want answers to, caffeine
or cocaine, bear meat

in the freezer. Sex. Unsleep. Talk,
incessant. And since when

do men not wear condoms,
not even ask you? Duvet corner

blackened by a candle. Scared
is only sexy for a second and only

if you're safe. He tells me
that after his brother died his mother

found the stash, drove around town
delivering packages to his customers,

asking for stories about her son.
He stands naked in the kitchen, sends

the switchblade singing past
my head. In the bathroom

I haul up all the red wine I drank
at the Canucks game while not

pretending to know the first thing
about hockey, not pretending

I didn't want to kiss him
and hit him equally because he did

and didn't remind me. Or maybe
it was the whisky. The blade

nose down in the IKEA coffee table,
flickering. We're all equal parts danger

and vulnerability. I ask how long ago
his brother died. He says,

I used to throw competitively. Jerks
the knife out from the centre of his life.

GREY AREA

In my defence, I was negged.

My body was flashing.

His chest.

Not everything he said about my poetry was insulting.

I understood what was happening.

I thought maybe if our two bodies came together.
Maybe if we kissed.

It was a shitstorm of politics. It was a tourist town
in the mountains. We were warned to look out
for elk and grizzly bears.

I wasn't scared.

I wasn't me that night. I was someone called Roxanne
in a club called Hoodoo.

In his defence, the gold sequin dress.

My body was a beacon, a gateway, a system
drunk on Hennessy.

He was drunk too.

I felt safe with him at first when we walked home
through the cemetery.

I thanked him.

I abandoned my body.

I thought sex was a kinder universe we could slide
into, borderless.

In his hotel room a small ball of power blazed
and I couldn't tell if it was mine or where it came from
but it was cold outside the circle in my defence and so I stayed.

I CAN'T FIND THE HEARTBREAK EMOJI

Vancouver keeps shading itself in the same-old
grey so I travel Craigslist on my smartphone

to a city I've never seen. Phoenix Missed Connections,
where hope bolts around on a dusty motorcycle,

searching more often than not for someone
named Hannah: Hannah from Home Depot,

Hannah in short shorts stealing $50 bills.
Beautiful Hannah with the Weird Dreams. Hannah,

who are you? And in asking I ask who am I
to be cruising this particular Craigslist,

wondering about you from two thousand miles away
in Vancouver? I like these stories better

than those on the news. Folks all over the world
are looking for each other. Is this the tender soul

of technology? OpenStreetMap, zoom out
on the lithium-green Anthropocene,

oil bunkers, clear-cuts, technofossils
reinforcing China's coastline while heaps

of seized ivory blaze in the hands of
Kenyan authorities. I suppose

it's safe to love Hannah. Love,
irradiant. To retreat, survival. To ascend

again and again in my pretend Phoenix
with Hannah, ask her how much she loves

elephants, if she's also a Gemini. What does
she dream of? Does she wake up crying?

Hannah on a porch swing, Hannah
in her phone light, sipping scorpion tequila.

Darkness flings itself around the shoulders
of the mountains. She types my name into the night.

NATURAL HISTORY

You swallow the poem
with your iron tablets, feel her

move your hand to the curtain,
to the candle, to your sadness.

She knows where to press.
She knows where you billow

like a crescendo of armholes,
where anxiety manifests

as skate blades scraping stone.
Where you leave the heat

of your body to grieve
and worry about

money. She bends you
at the clutch, cuts your breath

so you know what it's like to finish
but you'll never finish her.

SPOTIFY MY BODY

night windows virtuoso
complicit face
in the crowd ghosting heart like
a levee jaw like
a mirror loves a hammer love
me harder love song it goes on and on lost
in the light incomplete
and insecure creation's daughter's ribs utilities
civil twilight I like it
shallow I like it free I like it
impossible deep thunderstorm
of its own kind
wild thoughts Jesus, etc.
body of years still
young body say bravado say
my name all night loud

KENORA, UNORGANIZED

The pipes freeze, car won't start. Dad splits wood and Mom
KonMaris the closets to make space for me.
I borrow Sorels, shovel
hopeless trenches

through the unorganized territory of my childhood. This minus fifty
has some mercy, says CBC, meaning death
for larvae of the emerald ash borer,
a pretty but evil

invasive beetle that kills trees. Blessed is the junco at the feeder
who's not supposed to be here this time
of year. Blessed also the unlikely
swallowtail butterfly

found alive in a local man's garage. I've come here to collect stories
from my ancestry, but I keep procrastinating.
Watch my mind chase a jackrabbit
across the frozen lake,

which is a kind of cemetery. In (null), Ontario, you can hear the snap
as Tinder breaks. Radio waves roll into an empty sky:
There's no one around you. Evening,
I rewatch *Matilda*

with my parents, remembering a man I once loved who wept
passionately when we watched it together, he so
believed in telekinesis. Natural history,
strange and miraculous,

thistle seeds stirring under snow. Loneliness is its own magic, the way
the earth makes room. Mom flicks off lights
so we can see the wolf moon
turn red behind

a quiet grove of ash trees.

CROSSROAD

You may feel very familiar with the place
at the very first moment like you knew it before
or feel somehow that you own it
—Airbnb host

ok so now i see there's
loneliness either way

& also love & death
i am learning

to inherit myself
i am learning to connect

like when he messages me:
turn left at the chapel right

at the tree answer a riddle
about the light blink twice

at the shabby cat hunkered
under a dumpster acknowledge

your hunger this is your
yellow house this is your

blue door he says search
the brown coffin

for an ethernet cable
i say is that a metaphor or

SELF-PORTRAIT AS OSTRICH

After dancing endorphins
     brighten me

like a lamp or an ostrich
     lifting its head

I gave someone up for this self-
     embodiment Erin

on the phone says maybe
     your daemon

is an ostrich that gawky femininity
     that angry little face

Two a.m. I'm watching YouTube videos
     of ostriches mating

mercurial as ballet awkward
     as any sex act

I feel oddly solaced Google:
     ostrich symbolism

click *Egyptian mythology*—when
     someone died

their heart had to weigh less
     than an ostrich feather

or they couldn't go to heaven
       Humans shame

each other in so many creative ways
       Sunsigns.org says

see also: *Do These Three Things*
       to Be Happy

see: *Tarot Card Meaning—*
       Five of Wands

Home Remedies for Facial Paralysis
       see: *Understanding*

the Leo Man see: *Fertility*
       Erin says maybe

you're ovulating I do dream regularly
       that I'm gathering eggs

and I thought it was because I used
       to look after children

or because I've rewatched
       Fly Away Home

so many times and maybe that's true
       but maybe also

I'm finally taking responsibility for me
       Anger has a shape too

ditto shame ditto pride when it unfurls
　　　　　when I rise

up off my knees to become
　　　　　the biggest bird alive

THE FALLING MAN

Mary Oliver tonight I find myself

in another strange corner

of the Internet

where the man is still falling

seventeen years later

and in January

Outside my window

the prairie sun flushes drunk

and stumbles home shivering past

the airport

Curiosity keeps me clicking

keeps me noticing

the smoke reflected

in the glass

the way the man hovers in time

like a still of an osprey

wings tucked in

like maybe moments later

he flicked up out of some silver lake triumphant

with a fish

You died today Mary Oliver

while I was at the bank

I was angry

I'm often getting angry about money

When something happens

it's the feeling before

the feeling that snags

Dark now

but I don't close the curtains

Snow rosy under streetlight

This is a photograph of a man dying

the pull quote reads

A photograph of every witness

to this instant

strobing with life

It has nothing to do with you Mary Oliver

except proximity within me

the imaginer

except maybe some

kind of flight

The epigraph for section one is from Tess Gallagher's poem "Words Written Near a Candle" from *Under Stars* (Graywolf Press, 1978).

"Repeat Offenders" was inspired by my father's account of living and working as a new doctor in Churchill, Manitoba, and refers to the death of Thomas Mutanen, killed by a polar bear in 1983.

"Chihuly's Mille Fiori" was written after glass sculptor Dale Chihuly's exhibition *Utterly Breathtaking* at the Musée des Beaux-Arts Montréal, 2013.

The epigraph for section two is from Lucille Clifton's poem "sorrows" from *Voices* (BOA Editions, 2008).

"Three Days and the Next However Long" was written in conversation with Ellen Bass's poem "What Did I Love."

The epigraph for section three is from Rhea Tregebov's poem "Shift" from *(alive): Selected and new poems* (Wolsak & Wynn, 2004).

"This Little Girl Goes to Burning Man," "Crystals" and "Kenora, Unorganized" take structural inspiration from Ken Babstock's poem "Carrying Someone Else's Infant Past a Cow in a Field Near Marmora, Ont."

"Hippocrene" is written after John Steffler's poem "That Night We Were Ravenous" from *That Night We Were Ravenous* (McClelland & Stewart, 1998).

"Matrilineal" includes lines from Mary's Song of Praise: The Magnificat, Luke 1.

"Goodbye" was written after visual artist Patricia Piccinini's exhibition *Curious Imaginings* at the Patricia Hotel in Vancouver in 2018.

"Grey Area" takes inspiration from Cristin O'Keefe Aptowicz's poem "Not Doing Something Wrong Isn't the Same as Doing Something Right."

The epigraph for section four is a quote from the Twitter account Astro Poets (@poetastrologers), astrology by poets Dorothea Lasky and Alex Dimitrov.

ACKNOWLEDGEMENTS

These poems were created while living as a settler on the unceded, ancestral land and waters of the Squamish, Tsleil-Waututh and Musqueam Nations, as well as the territories of the Anishinaabe of Treaty 3 and Treaty 1, and as an uninvited visitor to the islands of the Hawaiian people.

Profound gratitude goes to Rhea Tregebov, my poetry godmother. To Canisia Lubrin and Karen Solie for mentorship, inspiration and advice during the creation of this book. Thank you to Erin Kirsh and Joelle Barron, long-standing first readers, favourite poets and dear friends. Thank you to the Nightwood team, especially Silas White, for your passion and dedication, and for believing in this book.

This book was made possible through the support of the Canada Council for the Arts, the BC Arts Council, the Banff Centre and the Writers' Trust of Canada. I am grateful to the editors and jurors that first gave these poems homes:

Grain Magazine: "What Blue"
PRISM international: "A Synonym for Oracle"
The Fiddlehead: "Crossroad," "Self-Portrait as Ostrich," "Natural History"
The Maynard: "Matrilineal"
Room Magazine: "Pue'o," "Camels in the Cariboo," "Hippocrene"
Contemporary Verse 2: "Crystals"
The Dalhousie Review: "Sun Valley Lodge"
The Puritan: "This Little Girl Goes to Burning Man"
Prairie Fire: "Garage Sestina," "Circles, Strokes"
FreeFall Magazine: "Finlandia"
Arc Poetry Magazine: "Chihuly's Mille Fiori"
Event: "Overnights at the Hospital," "The Boy Next Door"
Best New Poets 2014 (University of Virginia Press): "Repeat Offenders"

Gratitude to the Writers' Trust of Canada, Carolyn Smart and judges Jordan Abel, Sue Goyette and Emma Healey for nominating a selection from *None of This Belongs to Me* for the RBC Bronwen Wallace Award for Emerging Writers in 2019. I am humbled and honoured to be a part of Bronwen Wallace's legacy.

"Crystals" won *CV2*'s Young Buck Poetry Prize in 2017—thank you to the judge, Michael Prior—and was later selected for *The Best Canadian Poetry 2019* by Rob Taylor. Many thanks.

"This Little Girl Goes to Burning Man" was runner-up for *The Puritan*'s Thomas Morton Memorial Prize in 2017. Thank you to the judge, Suzanne Buffam.

"Hippocrene" won second place in the *Room* Poetry Contest in 2017. Thank you to the judge, Jónína Kirton.

"Finlandia" won second place in *FreeFall Magazine*'s Poetry Contest in 2016. Thank you to the judge, George Elliott Clarke.

Thank you to WKNDRS, Rachel Rivera and Claire Ouchi, for creating the artwork for the book cover of my dreams.

To my workshop peers, from UBC and beyond: your wisdom is in these pages. Thank you, thank you.

This book is dedicated to my parents, Darlene Hiebert and Vern Sawatzky, and to my siblings, Bram and Rachel, with deepest love and gratitude for my life. Thank you also to my sister Vanessa Rosewood, and to my sister-in-law Adrienne Toye. With gratitude to my ancestors for their sacrifice and ever presence. Thank you to B for the great adventure. To my chosen family, dear friends, co-creators and fellow dreamers—especially Erin Kirsh, Joelle Barron, Reece Cochrane, Erin Stainsby, Cara Kauhane, Emily Carlaw, Kyla

Jamieson, Alessandra Naccarato, Selina Boan and Danie Major: you make belonging feel possible.

To Adrick Brock: thank you for your curiosity and open heart and for reimagining home alongside me.

And finally, to you, reader, boundless thanks for giving these poems the opportunity to land.

Photo Credit: Molly Sjerdal

ABOUT THE AUTHOR

Ellie Sawatzky is a writer from Kenora, Ontario. She was a finalist for the 2019 Bronwen Wallace Award for Emerging Writers, and the recipient of *CV2*'s 2017 Young Buck Poetry Prize. Her work has been published widely in literary journals and anthologies such as *The Fiddlehead, PRISM international, Best Canadian Poetry, The Matador Review, Prairie Fire, The Puritan* and *Room*. She holds an MFA in creative writing from the University of British Columbia, and lives in Vancouver. *None of This Belongs to Me* is her debut poetry collection.